A Rookie Reader

Generous Me

WRITTEN BY MARY E. PEARSON
ILLUSTRATED BY GARY KREJCA

Children's Press®
A Division of Scholastic Inc.
New York • Toronto • London • Auckland • Sydney
Mexico City • New Delhi • Hong Kong
Danbury, Connecticut

Rookie READY TO **LEARN**

Dear Parents/Educators,

Welcome to Rookie Ready to Learn. Each Rookie Reader in this series includes additional age-appropriate Let's Learn Together activity pages that help your young child to be better prepared when starting school. *Generous Me* offers opportunities for you and your child to talk about the important social/emotional skill of relating to others: sharing.

Here are early-learning skills you and your child will encounter in the *Generous Me* Let's Learn Together pages:

• Simple fractions
• Vocabulary
• Counting groups of things

We hope you enjoy sharing this delightful, enhanced reading experience with your early learner.

Library of Congress Cataloging-in-Publication Data

Pearson, Mary (Mary E.)
  Generous me / written by Mary A. Pearson ; illustrated by Gary Krejca.
    p. cm. -- (Rookie ready to learn)
  Summary: An older sister lists all the things she would willingly share with her
younger sister, such as her broccoli and her chores. Includes suggested learning activities.

  ISBN 978-0-531-26427-0 — ISBN 978-0-531-26652-6 (pbk.)

  [1. Stories in rhyme. 2. Sharing--Fiction. 3. Sisters--Fiction. 4. Humorous stories.]
  I. Krejca, Gary, ill. II. Title. III.Series.

  PZ8.3.P27472Ge 2011
  [E]--dc22   2010049910

CHILDREN'S PRESS, and ROOKIE READY TO LEARN, and associated logos are trademarks and or registered trademarks of Scholastic Library Publishing. SCHOLASTIC and associated logos are trademarks or registered trademarks of Scholastic, Inc.

1 2 3 4 5 6 7 8 9 10 R 18 17 16 15 14 13 12 11

My sister whines and whines.
She says it isn't fair.

She tattles to my mom
that I refuse to share.

There are lots of things
that I would give her—all for free!
Things that she could *have*
if she wouldn't bother me!

I would give her my broccoli,

my carrots, my sprouts,

Mom's wet mushy kisses,

and all my time-outs.

The warts on my elbow,

my homework,

my chores,

and when I'm grounded,
the staying indoors.

My broken night-light,

the scab on my chin,

my wet slimy slugs
in their old rusty tin.

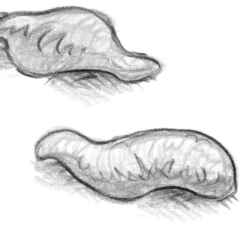

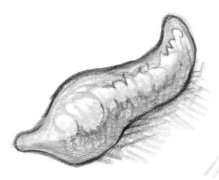

She says I won't share?
It just isn't true!

Why only last week,
I gave her the flu!

Congratulations!

You just finished reading *Generous Me* and learned the importance of sharing.

About the Author

Mary E. Pearson is a writer and teacher in San Diego, California.

About the Illustrator

Gary Krejca lives in Phoenix, Arizona, with his wife, Kim, their two dogs, Chester and Jocko, and their cat, Nick.

Generous Me

Let's learn together!

Sharing Together

(Sing this song to the tune of
"Yankee Doodle.")

Sharing together is such fun
It is generous to do.
Add in friends and laughter
To make a caring you.

Sharing together, keep it up.
Sharing is so dandy.
Mind your manners and show respect
And you'll be sweet as candy.

Sharing Will A-MAZE You!

The little sister wants her big sister to share her toys. Help her get the toys to her younger sister by following the maze path with your finger.

Share a Slice

Imagine you are sharing a pizza with friends. The pizza is divided into parts. A fraction is a number that names part of a whole, such as ½, ⅓, or ¼. Point to the slice that matches each fraction. An example is done for you.

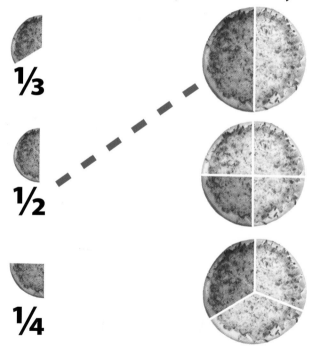

⅓

½

¼

PARENT TIP: The kitchen is a great place to have more fraction food fun. When you cut up an orange or bread for a sandwich, you can point out to your child that you are making fractions like halves and quarters. Additionally, using fraction words helps reinforce math vocabulary, such as: "Here is the one-half of an orange that you asked for."

I Can Share

The girl in this silly story shared things her sister didn't really want. It is nicer to share what your friends want. Say the missing words out loud to make up a story about sharing with a friend.

It is fun to play with _____.

name of friend or family member

I always share my _____   _____.

color   name of toy

I share my _____ and my _____.

name of toy   name of toy

We also like to play _____ together.

name of game or sport

That is sharing, too.

PARENT TIP: Young children are developing an increasing awareness of themselves. Their need to exert more control and decision making for themselves may lead to issues of ownership and sharing or not sharing. As children become more secure in knowing what is and is not theirs, they begin to more readily consider sharing with others. One way to help deepen this awareness is to relate sharing to something other than possessions. Sharing of ourselves — talents, skills, and even humor — helps children understand that there are many forms of sharing.

Sharing Silly Jokes

Now that you have read the funny story *Generous Me*, it is your turn to be funny. Share these riddles to get a laugh:

What has two hands and a round face, always runs, but stays in place? (A clock!)

What do you call a bee that is always complaining? (A grumble bee!)

PARENT TIP: Since many — if not most — children enjoy being funny, this activity can help your child see the relationship between sharing humor and being generous. For more laughs, you and your child can go to the library and ask your librarian to recommend some riddle and knock-knock joke books.

Count the Baseballs

The girl's friends are going to play baseball.

Point to each group of three baseballs. Point to each group of four.

Generous Me Word List (73 Words)

all	have	night-light	their
and	her	of	there
are	homework	old	things
bother	I	on	time-outs
broccoli	if	only	tin
broken	I'm	refuse	to
carrots	in	rusty	true
chin	indoors	says	warts
chores	isn't	scab	week
could	it	share	wet
elbow	just	she	when
fair	kisses	sister	whines
flu	last	slimy	why
for	lots	slugs	won't
free	me	sprouts	would
gave	mom	staying	wouldn't
generous	Mom's	tattles	
give	mushy	that	
grounded	my	the	

PARENT TIP: Find a word that begins with *S* in this list. Point it out to your child. Go back through the book and look for other *S* words. For an extra challenge, look for words in the book where *S* is in the middle or at the end of the word, such as *rusty*, *last*, and so on.